Splash!

Written by Ann and Karl Kralapp
Illustrated by Karl Kralapp

Published by Orange Hat Publishing 2018

ISBN 978-1-948365-36-9
Hardcover

Written by Ann and Karl Kralapp
Illustrated by Karl Kralapp

Orange Hat
PUBLISHING

www.orangehatpublishing.com

Married for almost 30 years, Karl and Ann Kralapp have been collaborators in every facet of their lives. Everything they did was better because they did it together. As a team, they raised their son, planned family events, coordinated children's programs at their church, taught, made meals, told stories, and wrote or illustrated. The two worked as one. Both were teachers for over 30 years. Karl taught elementary art, and Ann taught kindergarten. They love to create and tell stories for others, which they perform as the characters or using puppets. Ann is the "just do it" organizer and coordinator in their relationship, Karl the "let's make a plan and think this through." He is the creative, artistic part of their duo. With a love of storytelling, they share what they know and what is yet to be created as they journey through their lives together. Both are lifelong residents of the Green Bay, Wisconsin area, where they currently reside.

To Bob, Vicki, Diane, and Brian

FROG WAS SITTING ON A LILY PAD,
SOAKING UP THE SUN AND DREAMING
ABOUT PLUMP WORMS AND JUICY FLIES.

FROM BEHIND HIM CAME A **SPLASH** SO BIG THAT IT GOT HIM ALL WET AND SCARED HIM OFF HIS LILY PAD.

HE LANDED ON A ROCK AND LOOKED AROUND, BUT NO ONE WAS THERE.

FROG CLOSED HIS EYES AND
CONTINUED DREAMING ABOUT
BIG JUICY WORMS AND
PLUMP FLIES.

ONCE AGAIN FROG WAS AWAKENED BY A GREAT **SPLASH**, WHICH GOT HIM ALL WET AND SCARED HIM OFF HIS ROCK.

THIS TIME FROG LANDED ON THE SHORE. WHEN HE LOOKED AROUND, NO ONE WAS THERE.

FROG WENT BACK TO DREAMING ABOUT CREAMY WORMS AND CRUNCHY FLIES.

BUT ONCE AGAIN, FROM BEHIND
FROG CAME A BIG **SPLASH!**

FROG GOT SO SCARED THAT HE JUMPED INTO THE GRASS.

AS FROG LOOKED THROUGH
THE GRASS, HE SAW FISH.

FISH WAS JUMPING AND PLAYING AND
SPLASHING AND BRAGGING ABOUT THE
GREAT PRANK SHE HAD PLAYED ON FROG.

AS FROG SAT THINKING ABOUT HOW TO GET BACK AT FISH, A GUST OF WIND BLEW ACROSS THE POND. FROG SAW SOMETHING BIG AND WHITE FALLING FROM THE SKY. FROG WATCHED AS IT LANDED.

THERE WAS NO REASON TO BE AFRAID. IT WAS ONLY A WHITE PIECE OF PAPER. FROG GOT AN IDEA!

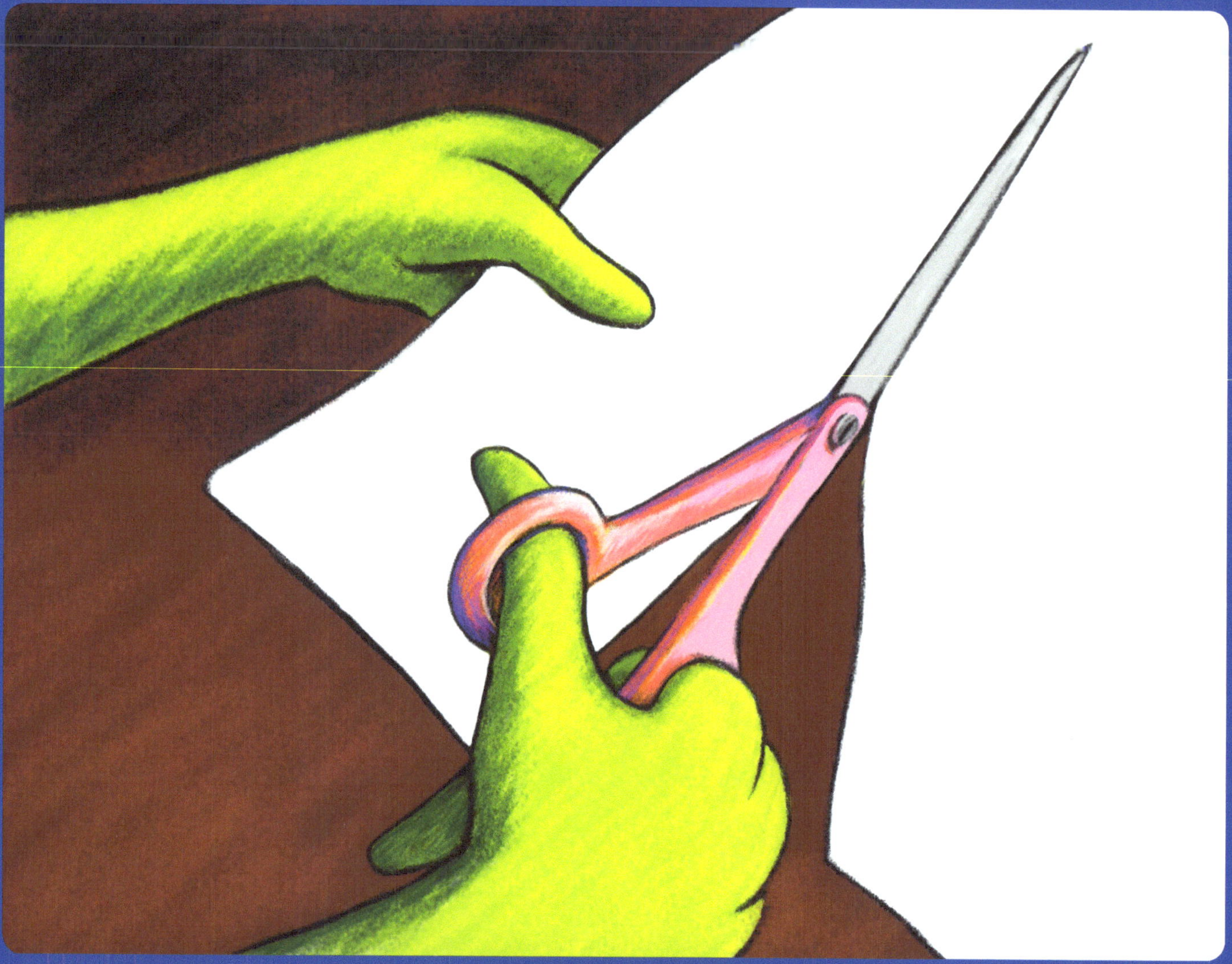

FROG TOOK THE
PAPER AND CUT
IT INTO A SQUARE.

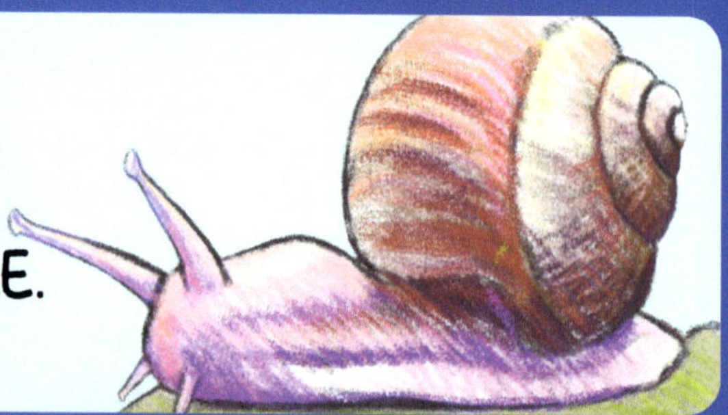

HE FOLDED AN ORIGAMI FROG JUST LIKE THE ONE HE HAD LEARNED TO MAKE AT SCHOOL.

NEXT, HE PAINTED THE ORIGAMI FROG SO IT LOOKED JUST LIKE HIM.

FINALLY, HE PUT THE ORIGAMI FROG OUT ON HIS ROCK TO SEE WHAT WOULD HAPPEN.

FROG SWAM BACK TO SHORE AND HID IN THE GRASS. HE WAITED QUIETLY FOR FISH TO COME. SOON FROG SAW FISH SWIM UP BEHIND THE ORIGAMI FROG.

SPLASH WENT FISH BEHIND THE ORIGAMI FROG. THE FROG GOT ALL WET. FISH WAS SURPRISED THAT FROG DID NOT JUMP AWAY.

FISH MADE AN EVEN HARDER **SPLASH**. THE ORIGAMI FROG GOT SOGGY BUT *STILL* STAYED ON THE ROCK.

SPLASH WENT FISH AS HARD AS SHE COULD. THE ORIGAMI FROG GOT SO WET THAT IT NOW COLLAPSED UPON THE ROCK.

WHEN FISH LOOKED UP, SHE WAS SHOCKED TO SEE THAT FROG WAS NOT MOVING. SHE BEGAN TO WORRY, THINKING THAT SHE HAD HURT HER FRIEND.

FROM BEHIND THE GRASS CAME LOUD LAUGHING.

FROG HOPPED OUT ONTO THE SHORE WITH A SMILE ON HIS FACE.

FISH WAS HAPPY TO
SEE HER FRIEND FROG
WAS OKAY.

FISH AND FROG HAD PLAYED BIG PRANKS ON EACH OTHER. IT WAS NOT FUN! THEY PROMISED NOT TO DO THIS ANYMORE.

BUT, NO ONE SAID ANYTHING ABOUT LITTLE ONES!

THE END

www.ingramcontent.com/pod-product-compliance
Ingram Content Group UK Ltd.
Pitfield, Milton Keynes, MK11 3LW, UK
UKHW061031310726
14089UKWH00009B/187
* 9 7 8 1 9 4 8 3 6 5 3 6 9 *